To tim,

All the Best,

Tara Torme

Humility is

A grace that's given by God

Always avoid pride

~ T K Torme

ALSO BY T K TORME

Ite Missa Est (Silver Bow Publishing)

Bull (Silver Bow Publishing)

In Conversation Vol I (Silver Bow Publishing)

In Conversation Vol II (Silver Bow Publishing)

In Conversation Vol III (Silver Bow Publishing)

In Conversation Vol IV (Silver Bow Publishing)

ITE, MISSA EST

VOL II

by

T K Torme

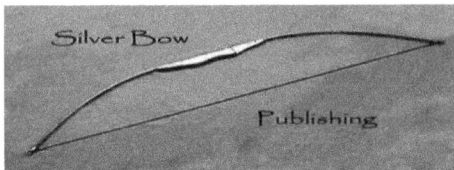

Silver Bow Publishing
720 Sixth Street, Box # 5
New Westminster BC CANADA

Title: Ite Missa Est Vol II
Author: T K Torme
Cover Art : 'Eden's Gate' painting by Candice James
Layout & Design: Candice James
Editing: Candice James

Wwwsilverbowpublishing.com
info@silverbowpublishing.com
ISBN: 9781774032497 paperback
ISBN: 9781774032503 electronic book
© Silver Bow Publishing 2023

Library and Archives Canada Cataloguing in Publication

Title: Ite, missa est. Vol. II / by T.K. Torme.
Names: Torme, T. K., 1977- author.
Description: Poems.
Identifiers: Canadiana (print) 20230152104 | Canadiana (ebook) 20230152112 | ISBN 9781774032497
   (softcover) | ISBN 9781774032503 (Kindle)
Classification: LCC PS8639.O79 I842 2023 | DDC C811/.6—dc23

FOREWORD

I highly recommend this book to everyone so they may better understand people with Asperger's who are not born with the social skills or given the social opportunities to connect with people easily and many times end up being unnecessarily marginalized by society at large They have much to offer and the better the world understands them the greater endowed the world will be

~ Candice James Poet Laureate Emerita
New Westminster BC CANADA

Dedication:

To His Holiness Pope Francis – the coolest Pope on the planet

To the priests and parishioners of St Mary's Parish in Vancouver

To William Murphy - the librarian at St Mary's Parish in Vancouver who has been super awesome in helping me learn more about the Catholic Faith Thank you so much for that

To Candice James whose editing of my book made the words shine

To Isabella Mori & Margo Lamont who have been super supportive of my writing

To St Scholastica my patron saint who has helped me write my haiku poems

St Scholastica watch over me

Ite Missa Est

What is true beauty

Your body the way it is

The way God made you

When I talk to God

I tell Him all my secrets

He listens to me

My Daily Missal

Gives me all of the sermons

For the Latin Mass

Pick one that suits you

For whatever your need is

There are different prayers

I would like to know

What is that day all about

Good Shepherd Sunday

Come to Mass with me

If you really do want to

Get to know me well

To go to heaven
Pure enough for my own soul
God please make me chaste

I would rather go
To Mass worship God all day
In all honesty

Totally sacred
Just to talk to God about
My special wishes

He is good and just
God is special to me: He
Is so powerful

He always listens
I can always talk to Him
God's always my friend

Since I was a small
Child I have always wanted
To be Catholic

Ite Missa Est

Answer all my prayers

Soften all my sinful ways

God enter my heart

I sleep through the night

My spiritual propofol

A night prayer I say

I wish I could wear one

The best thing that ever is

A priest in Cassock

God show me the way

What type of life do I lead

What's my destiny

I always use it

It is quite the epistle

My daily Missal

Friday devotions

I walked fast to get to Mass

I am out of breath

I really do love

That Priests do love their coffee

At Holy Family

In His own good time

He'll punish those who are bad

God is just and fair

He lives everywhere

Do you think that's possible –

God at the Opera

My favorite priest

Here at church Father Orlowski

Totally awesome

You always learn things

Listen to the homily

When you are at Mass

One needs a balance

Not everything has to be

A Catholic view

He'll listen to you

Worship any way you like

God comes in all forms

Take it up with God

If you have issues with the

Way I dress for Mass

God will still listen

I will pray my way it works

Just as fine for me

The best place is at

Mass if you want to catch me

That's where I hang out

Let me listen to

Your rhythm music for soul

God lives in my heart

Come one pass the wine

Priests acting behalf of God

Life of the Party

I've always wanted
To be of the Catholic Faith
Since I was a child

Listen carefully:
He is masked in messages
God speaks to us all

God is everywhere
Pulsating around the air
Feel the energy

Regardless of all
Our sins we are forgiven
God loves all of us

Show me light – not dark
Put into my heart love not
Hatred – faith not dark

Show us O Lord your
Kindness graft your salvation
O God give us life

My peace I give to

You: Reign God world without end

Peace I leave with you

I want to wash all

My sins in purgatory

When I'm dead and gone

God listens to you

Prayer will keep you calm in the

Most troubled of times

Don't be frumious

At God say your daily prayers

He listens to you

Be patient with Him

God is always there listens

To all of your prayers

How Sundays should be

To worship God and to sing

I love Sunday Mass

For my direct word

From God I go and look in

My Daily Missal

Perhaps He'll answer

If I pray to God and tell

Him my secret wish

Act accordingly

God is just and wise He knows

What is right for you

I'm better for it

To believe in God really

Helps me with my life

God spells them all out

Listen to all the secrets

Of the universe

It's the best place for

Your soul on Sundays go to

Mass to worship God

The people here are

Awesome great community

At Holy Family

Hear the rhythm of

The songs God is in my soul

Toe tapping music

Come on pass the wine

Priests acting – behalf of God

Life of the party

He will protect me

I have faith that I will be

Provided by God

He is there for you

Believe in God and see that

There is love around

My peace I give to

You: Reign God world without end

Peace I leave with you

Just by going to

Mass every Sunday I am

A better person

God doesn't like that

It's cruel and inhumane

Don't hit animals

How do you really

See me: Good; bad; horrible

Look into my soul

Slowly your mood will

Change for the better for all

If you go and pray

When you do eat with

Others to break daily bread

A meal's always great

Balance is everything

Faith is important but so

Are all my interests

Diversity rules

Mix with all people not just

The Catholic Faith

Sill learning the Faith

A Catholic in training

Call me CIT

He'll always be there

For me keep me safe from harm

Keep God in my heart

Still learning the faith

Learning all the prayers I am

A Catholic virgin

Masked under all the

Façades all kinds of people

Catholics – everywhere

Pure chaste virginal

Gold: a perfect element

Great Catholic metal

He is there for you

So talk to God about all

The problems you have

Still don't know the Mass

Reading my Missal I am

Still a virgin here

A seminary

Is a Father-In-Training

FIT for short

God lives in my heart

"Is God sexting you " You ask

In your twisted voice

Loves me from above

Always watches over me

My Guardian Angel

Heal me with your prayers

Anger sadness and despair

Oh God calm my heart

Major sin against

The Lord darkens your deep soul

To be frumious

You should go pay close

Attention during Mass time

Children do not fuss

Would He use Social

Media for all today

If Jesus were here

Does God approve this

A pyjama day relax

With nothing to do

Please do listen to

My prayer God can you hear me

Cleanse me from my sins

Be forever at

My side to light guard rule guide

Guardian Angel

Prayer group at Holy

Family calm and relaxing

Legion of Mary

Protects me from harm

With me always I keep my

Decade Rosary

From past childhood

You can find a faith hidden

Away quietly

Only way to go

To do Mass daily brings us

Much closer to God

Be closer to God

Escape to country live a

Much quieter life

I wonder about

Are communion wafers

Made with gluten

For the Latin Mass

My Daily Missal gives me

All of the sermons

In my daily life

It helps me to keep me focused

God is important

At Holy Family

I just love going to Mass

Every Sunday

Be much closer to

God you will be satisfied

Live religious life

Super natural

Visits God's message to us

Catholic Ghost Stories

My life in Your hands

God direct me as You see

Fit Your will not mine

Communion at Mass

Receive the body of Christ

Holy Eucharist

God is always there

When you pray the Rosary

Gives you good graces

God always hears

All your prayers you say to Him

Always keep the faith

God gives us the hope

To see that things will be fine

Never lose the faith

On the Rosary

Lie all of the mysteries

Gets you close to God

Humility is

A grace that's given by God

Always avoid pride

For all Catholics

Father Son and Holy Ghost

The Sign Of The Cross

Always after Mass

Worshipping here in God's House

Hanging out at church

What is modesty

To keep pure virginal chaste:

Femininity

When in confession

Confess all your sins to God

He will forgive you

Since I was small

Child I've always wanted

To be Catholic

Listen carefully

Father says a great lesson

In the homily

God is everywhere

Pulsating around the air

Feel the energy,

Masked under all the

Façades all kinds of people

Catholics everywhere

Supernatural

Visits God's message to us

Catholic Ghost stories

My life in Your hands

God direct me as you see

Fit Your will not mine

In God's Holy House

Worship prayer and attend Mass:

Holy Eucharist

Holy Eucharist:

Christ's body and blood in one

Dissolves on the tongue

In the morning say,

O my God I offer my

Heart and soul to you

The best way to talk

To God is the one that suits

Your mentality

God is always there

Seek Him out and you will seem

He'll answer your prayers

God sent you to me

Answer to a long time prayer:

My life in turmoil

True kind beautiful:

Was Jesus Christ Himself: Our

One Lord and Savior

St Scholastica:

A woman nun and her twin

St Benedict: Monk

You were sent to me

By God to help me in my

Deepest darkest hour

Call on St Michael

The Archangel for all your

Daily protection

God takes care of me

When I go and pray to Him

Every single day

When you are humble

God likes that and always will

Answer all your prayers

I cry unto you:

Lord please help: Deliver me

From my living hell

Blessed is the fruit

Of Thy Womb Jesus; Mary:

Holy; Mother God

Our Father Who Art

In Heaven Thy Kingdom come

As it's in Heaven

The sign of the cross:

Protects you everybody -

Every Catholic

If you've an issue

Take it up with God not me

I did nothing wrong

Oh Bless me Father:

These are all my confessions

For I've greatly sinned

Go to confession

Really is good for the soul

Free from all your sin

I put my trust in

God for all my daily needs

He'll take care of me

What is God's plan for

Me   I really do not know –

It's His will: Not mine

I am not blessed with

A life where my dreams come true

That is not God's plan

Where will God take me

What paths and plans are in store

It's His will NOT mine

Where will God lead me

To where He sees my calling

Life lessons to learn

A Scapular will

Protect you from any harm

Wear it all the time

God if you are there

Please do answer all my prayers

I really need you

God looks out for me

I tell him all my secrets

In my daily prayers

The Sign Of The Cross:

Say it every single day

God will protect you

Daily prayer does help

Whisper your troubles to God

He'll solve them for you

God is in my heart

Since I was a little girl

Keeps me safe from harm

Those who pray daily

Will have God close to their hearts

Their prayers get answered

A daily prayer will

Set you on the daily path

For doing God's work

Good morning Jesus:
Say this every single day –
It will change your life

Take care of every
Thing – Jesus I trust in you
I surrender all

God tells you what to
Do and say – your every move
You have no control

Nothing is just an
Accident: God has his say
In your destiny

Holy Family:
Jesus Mary and Joseph –
Pray to them always

To be Catholic:
True faith and the rosary –
THE COMPLETE BIBLE

Sweet heart of Mary,

Be my salvation My God,

I love you Save me

Anger and sadness

Towards all of my sad past

Sweet Jesus: HELP ME

God help me to find

Inner peace to my turmoil:

Anger from the past

God brought me out of

Westmount High School and right to

Sir Charles Tupper High

Mother Mary please:

Keep me in your most pure heart

Save me from my sins

Holy Eucharist:

Slowly dissolves on the tongue

God seeps in your soul

31

God help me to just
Survive in this horrid world:
I am in despair

My child come to me:
Confess all of your sins and
I will forgive them

The Sign Of The Cross:
Do this all the time to calm
Your anxiety

Married men can be
Priests - the other way around -
Priests cannot marry

What I really have:
Not imaginary friend:
God really exists

A true woman will
Cover her head during Mass
In God's Holy House

What is modesty

Covering up all your skin:

Not naked exposed

What's a true woman

One who accepts motherhood

Pure chaste virtuous

To find my true self:

Find me at the library

Or at weekly Mass

Be careful with words -

Never take Lord's name in vain:

Keep your language pure

Always during Mass:

Holy Eucharist on tongue:

Weekly homily

Confess all your sins

No matter how big or small:

You'll be forgiven

The Sign Of The Cross:

Father Son and Holy Ghost

Daily hug from God

A Priest's just a man

With feelings like you and me

Treat him with respect

A Hail Mary goes

A long way throughout the day:

Quick prayer on the go

To be grateful is

Your very breath in the air

God's great gift to you

God I'm in despair

I see no hope in my life

I crawl in my skin

A Priest who yells at you

To study your faith - I have

Great respect for him

My Christian name is

Not the one I was born with

But Scholastica

God's Holy water

Sprinkled amongst common things

Keeps you protected

Offer up to God

Every single suffering

He'll always bless you

Father forgive them

Why Hast Thou Forsaken Me

Commend My Spirit

At Holy Family

Children wear a veil at Mass:

Old fashioned values

Unless I tell you

I confess via Haiku

You will never know

St Anthony please:

Bless me today and always -

I really need you

St Anne please find me

A husband to marry 'cause

I want to be loved

Bring back tradition

To the daily Catholic Mass

The way it should be

St Scholastica

Please always watch over me

I need protection

At Mt Calvary

Jesus did die on the Cross

Passion Of The Christ

I only trust God

He does make much more sense than

Every day science

The Sign Of The Cross:

Father Son and Holy Ghost:

Holy Trinity

God please do help me:

Take away all of my pain

Heal me make me whole

Give God Reverence:

Bow your knee down to the Lord:

Show Him great respect

God I put my life

Into Your hands for You to

Direct towards Your will

Hail full of grace; blessed

Conceived: stainless soul thy birth

Lord abides with thee

'Jestic motherhood

Gratitude; great secret; heart

You're Heaven a part

Born: Our King Divine

Start celestial sign light

Rich poor will endure

Present to the Lord

Prophetic word; Simeon's sword

Servant now in peace

Marred by goading grief

Losing Christ; beyond belief

Amidst doctors; the boy

Gethsemane Christ's

Soul; grief anguish took their stand

Christ; that hallowed land

Stained in Christ that spot

Follow Him; Lot pillar; scourge

Lash His Life we merge

Cruel crown on His Head

Gold diadems of God Man

Power - best he can

Beauty of a tree

Carved wood destiny bear cross

Raise us from the dust

Crucified with Christ

Sacrifice; death; Satan's schemes

Christ on cross redeems

Rises glorified

Lives again walked among dead

Rise - our faith devout

Ascends into skies

Leave this earth; break human ties

Have Christ's promised place

On earth all grace pervades

Life's pleasure fades - seek out His Will

Every grace fulfill

Drawn to Love's embrace

Mother of God - Mary - entombed

Hope to be assumed

God's Queen - of Christ's reign

Crown celestial choirs

Bring peace victory

I still have not lost

My Catholic virginity

Still learning the Faith

I am really blessed

To live so close to my church

It's just down the street

I would rather pray

A Hail Mary every day

Than to get angry

I love to go to

Confession every Sunday

Highlight of my week

Since I was a child

I have always wanted to

Go to confession

Going to confess

Has been on my bucket list

Since I was a child

Whom O Lord Thou Dost

Create Hallow Quicken Bless

And give them to us

At Holy Family

Women put a veil on head

For the Holy Mass

Lord I can't even

Do this without you please help

Me with everything

God please take care of

All my issues - I need help

I can't deal with them

God I need you to

Take care of my issues: please

I give them to you

I long to wear a

Skirt to Mass and also be

Traditional girl

I just want to be

Traditional Catholic:

Wear a skirt to Mass

God I give you all

My pain that I suffer with

I suffer for you

God I give you all

My pain that I suffer with

I give it to you

Anglicans say Hail

Mary only on Sundays;

Catholics - every day

Can women be Priests

Never in the Catholic Church

But Anglicans can

Do Anglicans say
Father Son and Holy Ghost:
The Sign Of The Cross

I did not go to
First Friday Devotions Mass
I was too tired

God I'm in despair
Please help me to get rid of
All of my sadness

Be Thee God Father
Almighty in unity
Of the Holy Ghost

I am not the same
Person I was years ago
Since I went to church

I am more at peace
When I quietly sit at
Church worshipping God

If I say God Bless,

Does that make me fake unreal

Horrible person

If you wanted to

Go to a parking lot Mass

Just to worship God

God if you exist,

Why did you not reunite

Me with my father

For fast mail service

Go to Vatican City

To send your letters

You're supposed to pray

The Angelus Prayer at noon

Every single day

God why am I sad

Why am I never happy

Amongst my blessings

God please do guard my

Lips so that I speak no guile

Towards anybody

Please God help me to

Be always kind towards others

Never to be mean

God can you please help

Me to find a good husband

Who is Catholic

I give all my pain

To Jesus Christ Son Of God

For Him to deal with

God I want your help

I need you to fix my life

It's in Your hands now

Do Catholic Priests just

Wear pyjamas to bed or

Do they sleep naked

I would like to know

Would Jesus BBQ meat

Become pit master

God please do help me

I am in a lot of pain

I can barely walk

Hello God how are

You   Do you know who I am

Do you hear my prayers

I keep wondering

Why God gave me all this pain

I have every day

Do Angels exist

Do they only guard people

Or also creatures

God I want to know

Why did you let my father

Just abandon me

God please help me

Do make my day go smoothly

Please always bless me

God please do show me

A sign of the man I am

Supposed to marry

When I get married

I really want a Solemn

Nuptial Mass

I really do want

A Solemn Nuptial Mass

When I get married

How do Anglicans

Confess all their sins to God

Do they get penance

Confession's a cleanse

Scrubs your soul inside and out

A shining mirror

Every day I try

To read two verses of the

Catholic Bible

I miss Sunday Mass

I miss talking to the Priests

Sunday social time

God please make me good

Can you please help me with that

Do you think I'm good

Do other Catholics

Do The Sign Of The Cross when

They're on the toilet

God watch over me

Please keep my job safe and sound

That it's always there

Do Priests pick their nose

Do they fart in public to

Are they just like us

God can you help me

I don't want to be angry

Please help me keep calm

God do you hear my

Prayers   Do you listen to me

Will you answer them

Why do people need

A statue to pray to when

All you need is God

If Catholic Priests fart

During Mass will others think

It a new incense

God am I a freak

What is my purpose on earth

Why do I exist

God do you love me

Do you ever hear my prayers

Do you answer them

What if pandemics Are

God's way of getting rid

Of extra people

I am super stoked

Holy Mass is to resume

At Holy Family

God will I ever

Find myself a man who will

Want to marry me

God do you see me

Do you know that I exist

God do you love me

Church has changed my life

Made me a better person

Calmer to be with

God how can I deal

With all of this anger I

Have all of the time

God I need your help

I want to be pious chaste,

Humble virtuous

God help me keep calm

I do not want to be angry;

Push others away

God I want to be

The best person possible

Good pure chaste humble

God I look to your

Words for comfort and wisdom

Messages from you

Are you there God   It's

Me who really needs your help

Please answer my prayers

Let no unwholesome

Word proceed from your mouth but

Grace to those who hear

I can't wait for

Mass To be in God's House again

Amongst those I love

At church my quiet

Place where I can worship God

Receive Eucharist

My rosary is

All I need to get to sleep

Every single day

Just to be at Mass

Worship in God's Holy House

Hear His Holy Words

At seven am

People come to worship God

At Holy Family

God please help me

Find the strength to guard my tongue

Be charitable

Going to Mass gives

Me a sense of peace where

I'm always at war

God give me sunshine

My heart is always raining

Bitter saddened tears

God I do need you

All my anger and despair

Help me to calm down

God how I despair

All I have is bitter tears

Devoid of sunshine

God please point me

To the man I'm to marry

The man of my dreams

God please do guide me

To a good and honest man -

Weed out all the rest

Hi God how are you

I need you in my life now

I am in despair

God I really want

To get married: Please help me

To find my husband

God I do need you:

Please weed out all of those who

Are simply toxic

God I cling to you

For my daily salvation:

Save me from evil

God please weed out

All of the really weird men:

Keep only the best

God where are all of

The really good Catholic men

Are they in hiding

God's the only one

I could cling to when I've had

No one to talk to

Rosemary is just

The Rose Of Mary Mother

Jesus Son Of God

God come in my life

Please weed out all of the men

Who are simply weird

God please do help me

I really need your help right now

I am so messed up

God where on earth are

You when I really need you

Please do help me out

Oh God please help me

I need you to fix my life

Keep me free from sin

Did Jesus marry

Did he ever have a child

Just who was his wife

Anglican Priests are

Really super cool people

They get to say Mass

God I'm in despair

I am really scared right now

Don't know what to do

God I'm really scared

I am all alone right now

No one to talk to

How many times can

I say The Sign Of The Cross

Before I can eat

God I'm freezing cold

Would you please bring me some heat

I am shivering

I'm hungry for God

I crave for Him in my life

I need His guidance

I am so tired

Went to 7am Mass

And lunch with a friend

Do Priests pick their nose

Or do they fart during Mass

Do they also burp

Hi God how are you

How are you doing today

Can you be my friend

Don't want much in life

Just the pure simplicity

Humble pure and chaste

Early morning Mass

Peaceful and quiet at church

God is always there

Saying hello God

How are you doing today

I hope you are well

God are you up there

Are you listening to me

Do you see my heart

God please protect me

Always keep me safe from harm

Keep on blessing me

God what do you like

Do you like to eat chocolate

Do you drink coffee

The Traditional

Catholics are super picky

About the Mass form

God please watch over

My family and keep them safe

Make sure they are fine

God please guard my tongue

So that I do carefully

Choose in how I speak

Going to Mass is

The one place where I belong

Where I am at peace

Sundays are simply

Always going to a Mass

Relaxing and rest

God please hear my prayer

Help me to be more humble

Root out all my sins

Be silent in prayer

God will come into your heart

Pray the rosary

God are you up there

Do you hear my silent prayers

My sadness despair

God can you hear me

Do you listen to my prayers

When I talk to you

God please hear my prayers

Please do keep me safe from harm

Make me more humble

Why are women not

Allowed to become a Priest

In the Catholic Faith

Please God do help me

With my weight so that I do

Not gain any more

God please help me out

I am a really hot mess

Straighten out my life

It would be so cool

To be a Catholic Priest

And help out others

If I were a man

I would have become a Priest

And do all God's work

Ever since I could

Remember I've wanted to

Do all of God's work

God can you please tell

Me if I am forgiven

Of all my past sins

I would rather have

A simple humble wedding

At Holy Family

God please do help me

Become humble and simple

Honest and sincere

God please help me get

Married to a Catholic man

Who really loves me

God please do help me

I really want to marry

Find me a husband

My scapular is

Really itchy and scratchy

Don't like to wear it

Please God do help me

My feelings are out of whack

I always despair

Jesus who are you

You are such a mystery:

When is your birthday

Marriage is sacred:

Bond between man and woman

Covenant of God

God will you please help

Me with all of my issues

I am a hot mess

When I was a child,

I always longed to be at

Mass every Sunday

A baptism is

A way to cleanse your whole soul

Free from all your sin

God will I ever

Get married one day to a

Good Catholic man

Just what does go on

Inside of the rectory

Do Priests play board games

God be merciful

To me a sinner - please do

Forgive all my sins

God rewards those who

Always pray the rosary

Every single day

God please deliver

Me from all of my anger,

Sadness and despair

Ignorance - Scripture

Is ignorance of Christ which

No man can afford

The church is so hot;

Did they turn the heat on high

There is no fresh air

Lift up your hearts! We

Have lifted them to the

Lord Let us give thanks

If I brush my teeth,

Take the Holy Eucharist,

Do I brush again

Would I ever get

Cavities from taking the

Holy Eucharist

Rejoice in your hope,

Patient in tribulation,

Be constant in prayer

Crucified with Christ;

Is no longer I who live,

Christ who lives in me

God I'm really sad

Please take away my sadness

Help me to be whole

God help me to get

Out of my miserable life

I just want to die

My own getaway:

Going to the library;

Pray the rosary

I may not pray my

Rosary but I always

Do keep them with me

As a Catholic,

Should we be spending our time

By watching movies

Should Catholics spend

All their time by praying and

Avoiding TV

God please help me to

Find a kind and gentle man

Who will marry me

Will I ever find

A good and kind Catholic man

Who will marry me

Would you ever pray

To God or read the Bible

While on the toilet

It's the Catholic Faith

That is the true religion

All others: shadows

Catholic Aerobics:

Best way to get exercise

While you are at Mass

Who is to say I

Won't look good in a cassock

If I were a Priest

How can the Priests be

Anything but super cool

They get to say Mass

When God knocks on your

Door answer it and let Him

Come into your life

Why do all people

Around the world do call God

A He and not She

My mind is on Christ:

The tears that I shed for Him:

Genuine and real

Would Jesus wear jeans

Would Jesus get a tattoo

What would Jesus do

To ward off evil

Just sleep with a Rosary

You'll be more peaceful

If God answers prayers,

How come my father left me

Never to be seen

God can you please tell

Me what I'm supposed to do

And direct my life

As a child I longed

For the Holy Eucharist

Attend weekly Mass

To lead a Holy

Life is what I have yearned for

Since I was a child

The true power of

A woman: Humility

Pray the rosary

All my Catholic thoughts

Were masked hidden as a child

Emerged over years

Women really should

Dress modestly humble: be

Like Mother Mary

I don't know if God

Ever listens to me when

I ramble my thoughts

It would be so cool

If I could have been a Priest

If I were a man

If I were a man

It would be so cool to have

Become Catholic Priest

Please don't talk to me
When I pray the rosary
I get distracted

God please help me to
Melt away my anger and
Sadness and despair

God please help me out
I have anger and despair
Please get rid of it

God am I alone
Do I have any friends   Or
Am I just despised

How I long for God
To take away my anger
Help me to keep calm

Father forgive me:
I have nothing but anger,
Sadness and despair

I would rather go

To early morning Mass and

Be closer to God

God do you think you

Could turn up the heat a bit

I am shivering

Hi God it's so cold

Could you please turn the heat up

To July weather

God wants women to

Dress modestly and be chaste

Not act like hookers

God I'm miserable:

I cannot see where you want

Me to go in life

Hi God how are you

Do you get insomnia

Are you just like me

Mother Mary please:

Get these thoughts out of my head

I'm going crazy

God: can you please help

Me to find my way in life

I am a lost soul

Prayer is of value,

If we are all of one mind:

Otherwise it's vain

Where does God call me

What messages does he say

To me every day

God it's me speaking:

I need help with my life now:

What's my vocation

It's hard to pray the

Rosary when people are

Playing basketball

I know my heart to

Be entirely Catholic,

French and Latvian

I love daily Mass

A place where I can be calm;

Be closer to God

God: can you please help

Me find a Catholic group where

I can make new friends

Early morning Mass

Helps me to see God clearly

He lives in my soul

How do Priests find time

To go to car races   I

Thought they were busy

God opens all the

Doors He wants us to enter:

Keeps the others closed

If Jesus did fart

Would his fart just really stink

What would it smell like

I want to serve God

But also want to marry

God: please help me out

Money cannot bring

You any joy happiness

Like being with God

I want to serve God:

Find a place of happiness;

Fill the empty void

God please point me to

Where I am supposed to go

In my current life

If it is God's will

For me to serve God then He

Will send me a sign

It does give me great

Comfort to know people are

Praying just for me

The greatest gift you

Can give me is pray for me;

Look after my soul

I would rather spend

All my time with Nuns or Priests

For a grand old time

There is no place I

Feel more at peace when I am

At Mass and with God

A Catholic Priest

Who auditions in cassock:

British Pantomime

How can a Priest find

The time to play detective

He has to say Mass

Today's world does breed

Women to be immodest;

No belief in God

If more people did

Believe in God than the world

Would be much better

It is the belief

In God where one can gain strength

Learn the rules of life

I stay away from

The vanity of the world

Live humble simple

All I really need:

To go to Mass pray daily

Books and rosaries

Modesty includes

Carefully choosing your words;

And covering up

It's my rosary

That I like to pray daily

That keeps me focused

One should just never

Ever attend Mass without

Putting a bra on

What keeps me focused

Is praying my rosary

Every single day

The Lord be with you

Et Cum Spiritu Tuo

And With Thy Spirit

My garden is not

My personal getaway;

Going to Mass is

Unacceptable

To wear a nightgown to Mass

Way to casual

Would God mind that I

Do wear my nightgown to Mass

Or I get dressed up

I want to live at

Church where I am most at peace:

Be closer to God

Kneeling causes pain

When I take the Eucharist:

Sacrifice for God

Deus Vult: God Wills

To bear our crosses daily

Jesus in our heart

Have you ever heart

Of a Catholic Priest who wears

A soap opera beard

One would never think

Early morning Confession

Would get quite busy

God did not want me

To confess my sins today

I just have to wait

How did Father Brown

Become a good detective

As a Catholic Priest

You don't want to know

The countless prayer cards I own

That I never use

My bookshelf is filled

With all of the Catholic books

That I've bought at church

It amazes me

How many people come to

Early morning Mass

Saying your prayers on

The toilet will help you with

Your constipation

How can one deny

God's creatures are kinder than

Human beings on earth

Catholics do have

Teething rosaries for all

Their children of faith

Should Priests be drinking

Straight out of champagne bottles

At family weddings

There was a woman

Called Joan who became a Pope

A long time ago

Sometimes I don't brush

My teeth when I go to Mass

Early in the day

Catholics are to

Eat fish only on Fridays

Avoid all red meat

Would Jesus drive a

Bright red convertible or

Would he take transit

It's important that

I carry my rosary

With me everywhere

A Priest is just a

Social worker with collar

They do help people

God give me strength

Please help me to keep my peace

Take away anger

St Nicholas caught

A serial murderer

Who killed the children

There is a Catholic

Bishop of the moon who does

Have reign on the moon

I just cannot fit

Another rosary in

My tiny God Box

Many Catholics

Own more than one rosary

For their daily prayers

Natural order:

Men protecting the women

Take care of family

I can do all things

In Christ who does strengthen me

Every single day

Catholics rule the world

JFK was President

He was super cool

Hi God how are you

Did you have a fart today

How is Jesus Christ

Prayer keeps me focused

Gets me not to think about

Constant pain I have

If you want to know

Why my teeth are so crooked

Ask God and Jesus

The rosary can

Be the perfect distraction

From the constant pain

To be Catholic:

Imitate the life of Christ;

Be joyful always

It has been said that

A lay man can become Pope

In the Catholic Faith

Many Catholics have

More than one prayer book with them

When they are at Mass

The Sign Of The Cross:

Known to every Catholic

All around the world

I love tall people

Was Jesus Christ ever tall

How tall was Jesus

Are Cappuccinos

Named after the Cappuccin

Monks in Italy

Jesus Christ is just

One of the coolest people

He's a superstar

Just to read a bit

Minute meditations for

Every single day

In the Catholic Mass

Only organs should be used

Along with plain chant

84

The Mass should be said

In Latin for clarity

And accuracy

If it were not for

Me becoming Catholic

I'd be more angry

Iona's the birth

Place of Christianity:

Island of Scotland

God gave me the gift

Of writing haiku poems

To share with others

I wonder why the

Holy Eucharist tasted

Quite a lot like soap

I carry way too

Many prayer books with me when

I go to the Mass

At seven am

The Church is quite filled up for

Early morning Mass

Would Jesus be mad

At the current state of the

Church in today's world

As a Catholic

I am only supposed to

Eat fish on Fridays

If Jesus was here,

Would he have gone dyed his hair

Do a fashion trend

Many Catholics do

Carry a lot of prayer books

When they attend Mass

True humility

Something that I struggle with

Every single day

Read lives of the Saints

You will find some cool people

Who once walked the earth

Early morning Mass

Gets my day focused on God;

Meditate on prayers

Mass keeps me focused

Constant daily thoughts on God

Calm peace neutral

My Guardian Angel

Works overtime just for me;

Keeps me safe from harm

God is there for me

Meditate on God daily;

Pray the Rosary

It seems to me that

Most of the world's religions

Pray towards the East

I would never want

To be modern I'd rather

Be traditional

I would rather be

A Nun wear a veil and

Be humble modest

I keep wondering:

Did Jesus have allergies

Any health issues

God is my solace:

Gives me comfort when I am

Ever in despair

Catholic values are

The best way to live your life;

Good moral values

God hides small treasures

For people to discover

All around the world

Just a simple prayer

Is all you need to talk to

God every day

Use your own voice and

Simple words to talk to God

That is all you need

Be forever at

My side to light guard rule guide

Guardian Angel

Somehow Catholics

Really love Lord Of The Rings

And CS Lewis

God please help me to

Keep a close watch on my mouth

Help to choose my words

God whispers to me

Telling me how I should pray

Guides me through my life

It's God who directs

Us in our everyday lives;

We have no control

Car Rosaries are

Common amongst Catholics

You can pick them out

The Traditional

Latin Mass seeps into your

Soul - lives in your heart

Nothing gives me more

Pure joy than going to the

Weekly Latin Mass

There is nothing more

Awesome than hearing the true

Gregorian Chant

God cleanses the world

Through fires floods hurricanes;

New ghosts to battle

God waters the earth

Cleanses the world from all sin

Render it pure

Pills are never the

Answer to anxiety;

The Rosary is

I secretly do

The Sign Of The Cross in the

Small palm of my hand

Intimacy should

Only be saved for marriage;

It's a sacred act

Sweet Jesus please show

Your mother to mine comfort

Mine calm her worries

Let all bitterness

Wrath anger clamor slander

Be taken from you

God take away all

Negative thoughts memories;

Deal with them for me

It was God who called

Me to the Catholic Faith

Since I was a child

Jesus easily

Sticks to the roof of my mouth;

Peanut butter mouth

The Catholic Faith:

The only true Christian Faith

All other Faiths: Ghosts

God give me the strength

To always keep cool and calm

Amongst all anger

The world forgets Christ:

Wars the world disharmonized

World peace; just a ghost

It's elephant bones

That have launched our Protestant

Reformation here

Catholics have teething

Rosary rings for babies

Weird Catholic products

God's responsible

For everything that I do

In my daily life

Catholics are wise

When they say intimacy

Be saved for marriage

I am so hungry

I can eat a Crucifix

And the Eucharist

Forget blingy jewels;

Just give me a rosary

That belonged to you

My happy place is:

Writing haiku and chilling

Pray the rosary

Halloween really

Is a Catholic holiday

An old tradition

It's the quietness

Of the early morning Mass

That refreshes me

St Anthony please

Put the man I'm to marry

Right in front of me

Virility should

Be praying the rosary;

Go to Sunday Mass

It's my rosary

That I cling onto daily

For some peace and calm

A layman can be

A Pope of the Catholic Faith

Not just Cardinals

Good King Wenceslas

Looked on the Feast of Stephen

Deep crisp and even

I wish I could be

That person who invites the

Priest home for supper

I don't want to be

Liberated I want to

Be traditional

Father Geddes banned

The whole parish from singing

At the Sunday Mass

It's the Latin Mass

That keeps God's word all Holy;

Traditional form

Stay for the whole

Mass Judas left the Mass early

Don't be like Judas

Catholic therapy:

Going to confession and

Doing your penance

I don't like violence;

I like to pet kitty cats;

Pray the rosary

I can't go without

Books; writing; my Teddy-Bear;

The rosary; Mass

Pray the rosary;

Best form of meditation;

You don't need an app

The day is over

I can pray my rosary

And go right to sleep

No Catholic would be

Caught dead with a rosary

Made out of plastic

I am exhausted

I can't pray the rosary

My mind is foggy

God give me the strength

To go pray my rosary

So I can go sleep

Anglicans are just

A form of a Catholic light

Catholics - heavy

Gratitude just is

A breath that is in the air

God is all around

I try not to judge

But to see all of the sides

Be charitable

Ite Missa Est

Go the Mass is finished – come

Again next Sunday

All during Mass:

Sit kneel stand all while you pray:

Catholic Aerobics

The Lord be with you

Et Cum Spiritu Tuo

And With Thy Spirit

Would you rather have

No God and no peace or this:

Know God and know peace

There is a saying

That Jesus didn't tap 'cause

He loved to play Jazz

Humility; Grace

Brings you riches and rewards

Sent from God above

The power of prayer:

Get rid of unwanted thoughts

Take away your sins

Pray the Rosary

The words will help calm you down

The Rosary rules

While I am at Mass

All that sitting and kneeling

Daily exercise

God is an ointment

Itches when you put it on

Heals – makes yourself whole

Just say Hail Mary

Three times twice a day that will

Change your life around

Orange rosary

Brightly colored string of beads

Pray them every day

Let us all pray the

Rosary every day

Get in God's graces

Decade Rosary

Best way to say Hail Mary

Pray them every day

I keep my decade

Rosary with me always

Protects me from harm

Answers all your prayers

When you pray the Rosary

Whisper in your heart

Ten beads followed by

One for all those Hail Mary's

On the Rosary

Always mean your prayers

When you say the Rosary

Mary will be pleased

Pray the Rosary

Helps with your anxiety

Completely drug free

What's a Rosary

A great way to say your prayers

Every single day

God blesses those who

Always say their daily prayers

The Rosary too

Bright pink rosary

All the prayers upon the beads

Holy Eucharist

Answers all your prayers

When you pray the rosary

Whisper in your heart

God blesses those who

Always say their daily prayers

The rosary too

Pray the rosary

Always faithfully daily

It will change your life

This is my God Box:

All my rosaries lie here

For my daily prayer

Bring my rosary

Every single place I go:

A portable prayer

Pocketful of prayers

Always in my purse with me:

Holy Rosary

God does speak to me

Every day when I pray the

Holy Rosary

True manhood really

Is not macho but praying:

Holy Rosary

A rosary in

My purse every single day

Keeps me safe from harm

Just what is true strength

Pray the rosary always:

Makes you gentle wise

If you do pray the

Rosary every day you

Gain true inner strength

True inner strength comes

When you pray the rosary

Every single day

Holy Rosary:

Meditate upon the beads:

Soothing for the soul

True strength always comes

In praying the rosary

Not in lifting weights

The best defense tool

Is the mighty rosary

Pray it every day

A rosary will

Help to calm your busy mind

To keep you focused

A cold rosary

Can be pure hell to pray on:

A penance from God

A rosary can

Quieten the story mind

Prepare for battle

Daily prayer routine

Along with my rosary

Keeps me close to God

Daily rosary

Better than medications

Helps you sleep the night

I always keep a

Rosary with me - for my

Spontaneous prayers

For anxiety

Pray the rosary daily

Really calms you down

God calls to me when

I pray my rosary – my

Fingers on the beads

Between my fingers

Lay my rosary that I

Always pray daily

God is there for me

There on every single bead

Of the rosary

A nun's rosary

Touched by Holy fingers: God

Whispers on the beads

God whispers in my

Ear: Pray the rosary for

Your daily blessings

To be Catholic:

True faith and the rosary –

THE COMPLETE BIBLE

Sweet heart of Mary,

Be my salvation My God,

I love you Save me

Holy Eucharist:

Slowly dissolves on the tongue

God seeps in your soul

A true man will pray

The Rosary every day

Protects his woman

A true woman will

Cover her head during Mass

In God's Holy House

A real man eats meat;

Goes to Mass every Sunday:

Prays the rosary

Always during Mass:

Holy Eucharist on tongue:

Weekly homily

To be Catholic

Means praying the Rosary

And going to Mass

After I pray the

Rosary; I fall asleep:

Calm and peaceful rest

A Hail Mary goes

A long way throughout the day:

Quick prayer on the go

Pray the Rosary

Every single day to fight

Your daily anger

To get rid of your

Daily anger every day

Pray the Rosary

I just cannot fit

All of my Rosaries in

My tiny God Box

Just a rosary

Prayer every day will help you

Be closer to God

Every Sunday at

Mass the Rosary is prayed:

God in every heart

I love rosaries:

Hail Marys upon the beads -

Soothing to the soul

Pray the Rosary

Every single day and you

Will always be blessed

I spend time alone

Just praying the rosary

Every single day

When I do not pray

The rosary every day

I just cannot sleep

I would rather pray

A Hail Mary every day

Than to get angry

A rosary will

Really help to calm you down

Lowers blood pressure

When I do not pray

The rosary every day

I become anxious

I love to go to

Confession every Sunday

Highlight of my week

Father would you please

Bless my rosary for me

I'd really like that

Pax Domini Sit

Semper Vobis Cum Et Cum

Spiritu Tuo

I am Catholic

I go to the Latin Mass

Pray the rosary

The line-up today

Was way too long for me to

Go to confession

I cannot resist

Buying books and rosaries

At Holy Family

Father Oballo,

Would you please go and bless my

Brand new rosary

Mini rosary:

Perfect way to say your prayers

Every single day

Nestled in my hand

Lies my mini rosary

A portable prayer

A portable prayer

Lies my mini rosary

Nestled in my hand

My rosary gives

Me comfort dries all my tears

Keeps me company

In my loneliness,

My rosary is really

My one only friend

Many Catholics

Own a lot of rosaries

For their daily prayer

I can only count

On my daily rosary

Prayers for company

A rosary is

The perfect Valentine's gift

For a Catholic girl

My God Box is chalk

Full of all the rosaries

That I've collected

I love to pray my

Rosary every single

Day It keeps me calm

If more people prayed

The rosary there would be

Less anxiety

I would rather pray

My rosary than to get

Angry at people

In the summer time

My rosary gives me prayers

Every single day

Every single day

My rosary gives me prayers

In the summer time

The only solace

I have is my rosary

No other comfort

Through Whom O Lord Thou

Create hallow quicken bless

And give them to us

God does reward those

Who do pray the rosary

Every single day

Many Catholics

Do keep a car rosary

For their daily prayers

Quick Sign Of The Cross

Keeps all evil things away -

Satan safe at bay

My life in God's hands

He directs me in my life

Life and death balance

Holy Eucharist

Memories of a distant past

God's House - a ghost town

Fresh Priest on the job

7 am confessions

Holy Family

Early confessions

Fresh Priest - Holy Family

In the crying room

God is now online

Public Masses have been banned

Communities divide

Where church pews were full

Now just a silent echo

God's House: A ghost town

God's house once was full

Now a shadow of itself

Ghosts that walk the halls

A true man is one

Who will pray the rosary

Every single day

To confess early

Wash away all of my sins

Clean for the whole day

Ite Ad Joseph

Go to Joseph for all things

He will keep you pure

Would you rather have

No God and no peace or this:

You know God Know peace

While I am at Mass

All that sitting and kneeling

Daily exercise

Ite Missa Est

Go the Mass is finished – come

Again next Sunday

Can I use Haiku

Poems to confess all of

My grave sins to God

Always watch over

Me or I will betray You

Just like Judas did

Be Thee God Father

Almighty in unity

Of the Holy Ghost

As a Catholic

I have lots of rosaries

For my daily prayer

Let us all pray the
Rosary every day
Get in God's graces

Decade Rosary
Best way to say Hail Mary
Pray them every day

I keep my decade
Rosary with me always
Protects me from harm

Answers all your prayers
When you pray the Rosary
Whisper in your heart

What's a Rosary
A great way to say your prayers
Every single day

God blesses those who
Always say their daily prayers
The Rosary too

God's words are upon

The beads directing your soul

Pray the rosary

Answers all your prayers

When you pray the rosary

Whisper in your heart

Pray the Rosary:

Your life will start to change round

Blessings are abound

God gives graces to

All who pray the rosary

Every single day

God blesses those who

Always say their daily prayers

The rosary too

Pray the rosary

Always faithfully daily

It will change your life

Pocketful of prayers

Always in my purse with me:

Holy Rosary

God does speak to me

Every day when I pray the

Holy Rosary

True inner strength comes

When you pray the rosary

Every single day

Holy Rosary:

Meditate upon the beads:

Soothing for the soul

God is there for me

Always on each single bead

Of the rosary

Orange rosary

Brightly colored string of beads

Pray them every day

A nun's rosary

Touched by Holy fingers: God

Whispers on the beads

A rosary can

Quieten the story mind

Prepare for battle

The best defense tool

Is the mighty rosary

Pray it every day

A cold rosary

Can be pure hell to pray on:

A penance from God

Daily prayer routine

Along with my rosary

Keeps me close to God

Daily rosary

Better than medications

Helps you sleep the night

I always keep a

Rosary with me - for my

Spontaneous prayers

God calls to me when

I pray my rosary – my

Fingers on the beads

God whispers in my

Ear: Pray the rosary for

Your daily blessings

All during Mass:

Sit kneel stand all while you pray:

Catholic Aerobics

A true man will pray

The Rosary every day

Protects his woman

A real man is kind;

Goes to Mass every Sunday:

Prays the rosary

Blessings all around:

Masked invisibility -

On the rosary

To be Catholic

Means praying the Rosary

And going to Mass

After I pray the

Rosary; I fall asleep:

Calm and peaceful rest

To get rid of your

Daily anger every day

Pray the Rosary

I just cannot fit

All of my Rosaries in

My tiny God Box

Every Sunday at

Mass the Rosary is prayed:

God in every heart

I love rosaries:

Hail Marys upon the beads -

Soothing to the soul

Pray the Rosary

Every single day and you

Will always be blessed

I spend time alone

Just praying the rosary

Every single day

When I do not pray

The rosary every day

I just cannot sleep

You always create

Bless bestow us all good things

Sanctify fill life

Passed: our lips as food

Possess purity of heart

Heal: eternity

A rosary will

Really help to calm you down

Lowers blood pressure

When I do not pray

The rosary every day

I become anxious

Father would you please

Bless my rosary for me

I'd really like that

Pax Domini Sit

Semper Vobis Cum Et Cum

Spiritu Tuo

I am Catholic

I go to the Latin Mass

Pray the rosary

Father Oballo,

Would you please go and bless my

Brand new rosary

Inside my God Box

Rest all of my rosaries

That I use to pray

Mini rosary:

Perfect way to say your prayers

Every single day

My rosary gives

Me comfort dries all my tears

Keeps me company

In my loneliness,

My rosary is really

My one only friend

I can only count

On my daily rosary

Prayers for company

A rosary is

The perfect Valentine's gift

For a Catholic girl

My God Box is chock

Full of all the rosaries

That I've collected

At seven am

Is the best time to confess

The Priest's really fresh

A rosary prayer

Is a really good way to

Always talk to God

When I go to die,

I would like to be buried

With my rosary

What better way to

Start the day than drink coffee

And pray rosary

Each time I go to

Church I get a warm hug from

Someone who loves me

He sat with sinners

And those others did condemn

Jesus didn't judge

Through the Word Of God

My Whale call gets stronger each

Time I attend Mass

Perhaps God wears a

Pair of Lederhosen and

Robin Hood Hat too

Maybe God wears Elf

Boots with pointed toes and bells

Ring when He appears

Feel the energy

Pulsating around the air

God is everywhere

Be humble grateful

They will bring you great rewards

More than worldly goods

God: please protect me

From all the evil spirits

Torturing my soul

God doesn't even

Care what bag I bring to Mass

Just that I worship

Put into my heart

Love not hatred – faith not doubt

Show me light – not dark

My heart: solid gold

Pure full and always ready

To receive God's love

Guardian Angel

Be forever at my side

To light guard rule guide

I forgive all who

Have injured me please pardon

All whom I've injured

Peace I leave with you

My peace I give to you reign

God world without end

Inebriate me

Water from the side of Christ

Good Jesus hear me

Oh God calm my heart

Anger sadness and despair

Heal me with your prayers

To kill somebody

It is wrong to take a life

That is up to God

When I'm dead and gone

I want to wash all my sings

In purgatory

To be frumious:

Major sin against the Lord

Darkens your deep soul

I want to go to

Purgatory – to wash away

All of my bad sins

How do I forgive

All who have badly injured

Me – too much to bear

Children – do not fuss

During Mass time – you should go

Pay close attention

Don't hit animals

It's cruel and inhumane

God doesn't like that

O God give us life

Show us O Lord Your kindness

Grant Your salvation

Regard not my sins

Deign to give peace unity

God world without end

Prayers will keep you calm

In the most troubled of times

God listens to you

Say your daily prayers

Don't be frumious at God

He listens to you

God is always there

Listening to all your prayers

Be patient with Him

God please make me chaste

Pure enough for my own soul

To go to heaven

Keep me from being

Angry at others – keep peace

With everybody

I want to be pure

And clean – deep right in my soul

To go to heaven

Toe tapping music

Hear the rhythm of the songs

God is in my soul

God live in my heart

Let me listen to your rhythm

Music for my soul

A pyjama day

Relaxing nothing to do –

Does God approve this

Take away your sins

Get rid of unwanted thoughts:

The power of prayer

God comes in all forms

Worship any way you like

He'll listen to you

I don't need to come

To every single church thing

To be Catholic

When you are at Mass

Listen to the homily

You always learn things

If you say your prayers

They help you to reflect on

Life – so work the prayer

Would priests attend any

Live theatre in their cassocks

Or stay home and pray

All those who have wronged

Others in their evil deeds

Will all get punished

If you say Hello

Eternal Loving Presence

God will come to you

Be professional

In the way you dress yourself

God also likes that

Can I use Haiku

Poems to confess all of

My grave sins to God

God enter my heart

Soften all my sinful ways

Answer all my prayers

I want to marry

Please God do answer my prayer

My heart's desire

Holy Family

Church – a special place for me

My new family

I really love God

He lives deep into my heart

He cares about me

Just to talk to God

About my special wishes

Totally sacred

I tell God what's deep

In my heart so that He will

Answer all my prayers

God is special to

Me: He is so powerful

He is good and just

I go and look in

My Daily Missal for my

Direct word from God

God put into my heart

Prepare me for a marriage

With that special man

Just to be courted

In such a Godly manner

Makes me feel so good

I pray every day

To God to help me to change

My old sinful ways

Ite Missa Est

I want to be pure

And chaste and free of my sins

Live a better life

Listen to all the

Secrets of the Universe

God spells them all out

Think negatively

And all you'll get in return

Devil in disguise

On Sundays go to

Mass to worship God: it is

Best place for your soul

Those who worship and

Pray have much happier lives

Than those in great sin

At Holy Family

The people here are awesome

Great community

Jesus fill my heart

With love hope and never hate

Heal me from my pain

I need to have God

In my life to keep me calm

He really loves me

Without God I am

Nothing but an angry soul

Full of hate revenge

Jesus heal my soul

Take away all of my sins

I want to marry

Listen to all the

Music at Holy Family

On Canada Day

Ask Father Marchand

Weekly sessions – of the Faith

Ask any question

Live religious life

Be much closer to God: You

Will be satisfied

What's my cross to bear

Why do I feel all alone

Do you love me God

The Catholic Faith

It's a complex religion

Goes way back in time

To be God fearing

Means to always respect The

Lord God from above

To pray every day

Gives you protection from God

Blessings from above

They will protect you

They also need the food too –

Share with Gods' creatures

Save me from my sins

God come into my life and

Make me whole again

Show us O Lord your

Kindness grant Your salvation

O God give us life

Water from the side

Of Christ good Jesus hear me

Inebriate me

Anger sadness and

Despair heal me with your prayers

Oh God calm my heart

AUTHOR PROFILE:

T K Torme was born Tara Kimberley Torme in Montreal, Quebec in 1987 and moved to Vancouver, BC in 1992. She received her B.A. in English in 2001. T K has been writing since she was a child and has always loved reading and writing poetry. It brings her great joy & relaxation and opens her mind to new possibilities allowing her to expand her thoughts and channel them from her mind to the page into poetry

T K has Asperger's Syndrome, and she finds poetry helps her to express her feelings with vision and clarity in concise words

CPSIA information can be obtained
at www.ICGtesting.com
Printed in the USA
BVHW050343270123
656873BV00005B/23

9 781774 032497